COURAGE IN HER CLEATS

The Story of Soccer Star Abby Wambach

*For my sister, Kristy, whose courage was established in cleats but now fills every fashionable
shoe she wears. For Liv and Mia: You inspire those around you, on and off the field.
For anyone who needs this reminder: Sometimes life is tough. You are tougher.*
—K. C.

*For my brother Marcu, a wonderful young man, hardworking athlete,
and the embodiment of perseverance.*
—A. B.

Text copyright © 2023 Kim Chaffee
Illustrations copyright © 2023 Alexandra Badiu

First published in 2023 by Page Street Kids
an imprint of
Page Street Publishing Co.
27 Congress Street, Suite 1511
Salem, MA 01970
www.pagestreetpublishing.com

Distributed by Macmillan, sales in Canada by The Canadian Manda Group

23 24 25 26 27 CCO 5 4 3 2 1
ISBN-13: 978-1-64567-629-4
ISBN-10: 1-64567-629-3

CIP data for this book is available from the Library of Congress.

This book was typeset in Amasis MT. The illustrations were done digitally.
Cover and book design by Melia Parsloe for Page Street Kids.
Edited by Kayla Tostevin for Page Street Kids.

Printed and bound in Shenzhen, Guangdong, China

Page Street Publishing uses only materials from suppliers who are committed to responsible and
sustainable forest management.

Page Street Publishing protects our planet by donating to nonprofits like The Trustees, which focuses
on local land conservation.

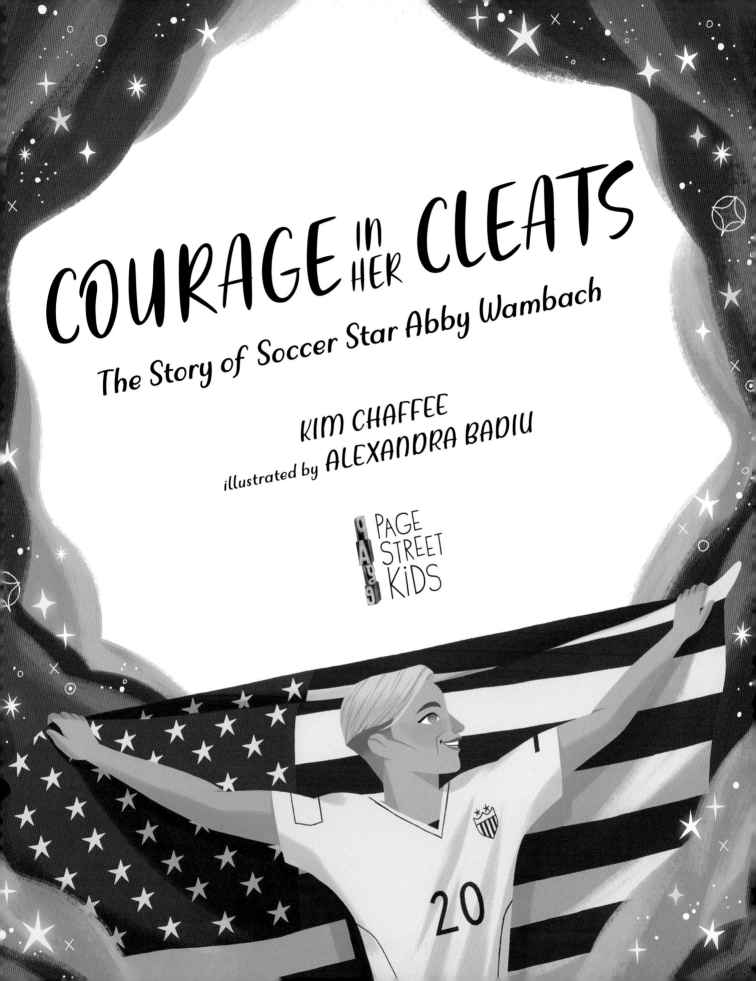

COURAGE IN HER CLEATS

The Story of Soccer Star Abby Wambach

KIM CHAFFEE

illustrated by ALEXANDRA BADIU

PAGE STREET KIDS

As the youngest of seven children, Abby Wambach learned quickly that to be heard, she needed to be loud and clear.

So she was *loud* when her brothers and sisters stole her french fries. She made *clear* her feelings on fancy dresses.

And she was loud *and* clear that she wanted to be part of any competition . . .

especially soccer.

thwump . . . thwump . . . thwump . . .

Like a compass in her cleats, young Abby guided the ball downfield, dancing and darting past defenders. As she neared the net, she pulled her leg back like a slingshot and released.

thwump . . . whizz . . . whoosh . . .

WIDE!

A wave of disappointment rushed through her. Missing goals was tough. But Abby was tougher. She shook off the miss and got back in the game.

In her senior year of high school, Abby and the varsity soccer team made it to the state championship. As captain for the Monarchs, Abby didn't want to let them down.

thwump . . . whizz . . . whoosh . . . GOAL!

Abby scored two goals. But, in a flash, the game was tied up.

Both teams battled into overtime. But when the Chiefs skirted the ball past the goalkeeper, Abby felt the game slip away.

Devastated, she dropped to her knees and wept. Losing big games was tough.

But Abby was tougher.

After graduation, she joined the University of Florida's women's soccer team. Ready to prove herself, Abby pushed through two, sometimes three, practices a day. During games, she continued to do what she did best: drive, strike, and boot the ball to the back of the net.

The coaches for the U.S. Women's National Soccer Team took notice.

But they weren't ready to sign her just yet. The rest of her game needed work. Especially her running.

Eager to earn a spot on the team, Abby met with Randy, a local trainer.

"You're leaving craters in the track," he said.

Her body was tense. Her energy was wasted. Randy showed Abby how to run lighter on her feet and relax her muscles as she moved.

Before long, her skills, speed, and stamina improved. The U.S. Women's National Team wanted her on the roster.

Abby couldn't believe it! She would represent her country!

But then, her doubts overshadowed her joy. *Am I good enough to play at this level? Can I keep up?* Pushing outside her comfort zone was tough.

But Abby was tougher.

The veterans were quick as lightning and knew exactly where to be on the field. Abby watched. She listened.

And soon . . .

thwump . . . whizz . . . whoosh . . . GOAL!

. . . she showed them what she could do.

Game after game, Abby and the team dazzled fans.

Corner kicks. Hat tricks. Dramatic late-in-the-game wins—like her header in the 2004 Olympics that won the team the gold medal!

As the years dribbled by, veteran players retired. Abby grew more confident in her cleats. In the huddle and on the field, Abby's voice took the lead, loud and clear.

"Every time you put on this jersey, it means something," she told them.
"We got this!"

Goal after goal, she pointed to her teammates, knowing she hadn't done
it alone.

In 2008, the Olympic Games were held in Beijing, China. Abby and the team couldn't wait to defend their gold medal. Before they left, they played one last exhibition game against Brazil.

It started out like any other friendly match.

thwump ... thwump ... thwump ...

Fierce and focused, Abby and the team raced like rockets up and down the field, crisscrossing the ball, fighting for possession.

Then, Abby charged, full speed, to meet the ball off a pass.

But Brazil's defender charged, too.

The players collided and Abby fell to the ground.

For a moment, she lay still.

Unable to get up, she signaled for the trainers and emergency crew. Abby's left leg was broken . . .

and so were her dreams of returning to the Olympics.

"I just can't believe this happened," said Abby, after four hours of surgery. "I don't get hurt. I can play through anything." Tears stung her eyes.

Soon, her worries turned to her teammates halfway around the world. It was game time. More than anything, she wanted to help. But how?

Abby opened her laptop and typed an email:

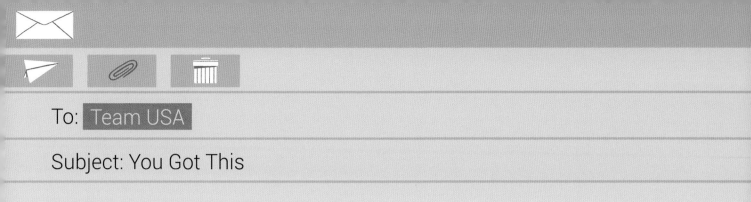

To: Team USA

Subject: You Got This

To the U.S. Olympic Women's National Soccer Team:

This is a team that will win gold, and you can't doubt that for one second. Yeah, you're going to make mistakes. Yes, you will be nervous. . . . It's not about what happens; it's about how you react to all of it. . . . You can do this. . . . Good luck and play your hearts out. I'll be watching.

—Abby

The team heard Abby loud and clear, all the way in China. They worked together, fought hard, and won Olympic gold again!

Back home, Abby fought hard, too. First, to walk again. Then to run.

She was determined to get back on the field. But building back her strength, speed, and stamina was the toughest challenge Abby had ever faced.

Would she ever be the player she was before?

One year and three days after her injury, in her second game after returning to the National Team, Abby played for a hometown crowd.

Late in the game, she slipped past two defenders and met the ball off a pass. With courage in her cleats, she neared the net, pulled her leg back like a slingshot, and released.

thwump...

whizz...

whoosh...

GOAL!

She scored her 100th career goal! There was no doubt about it. Abby was back!

And she was tougher than ever.

Abby's Impact on U.S. Women's Soccer

thwump ... whizz ... whoosh ... GOAL!

From the moment she laced up her first pair of cleats, Abby was a force to be reckoned with, dazzling spectators with her ability to score goal after goal. But for Abby, being on the U.S. Women's National Soccer Team and playing for her country was about more than the score. "As important as it is to score goals," she said, "it's also equally important to be a leader." Loud and clear with both her words and her actions, Abby demonstrated what it takes to succeed: grit, determination, and teamwork.

During her career on the U.S. Women's National Team, Abby scored 184 international goals; more than any other U.S. soccer player, male or female. She won two Olympic medals (2004, 2012), was named U.S. Soccer's Female Athlete of the Year six times, and was inducted into the National Soccer Hall of Fame. In 2015, just before she retired, Abby finally won the one major honor that eluded her: a FIFA World Cup. Just like at the end of her high school championship game, Abby dropped to her knees when time expired in the World Cup Final. Only this time, it was to celebrate a victory that took more than ten years to achieve.

Kid Cleats

*Abby was born on June 2, 1980, in Pittsford, New York, as Mary Abigail Wambach.

*Abby's older sister Beth introduced soccer to the Wambach family. When Beth wanted to learn to play, her family checked out a book about the sport from their public library.

*At age nine, Abby scored twenty-seven goals in three games and was sent to play in the boys' league.

*A signed poster of soccer legend Mia Hamm hung on Abby's childhood bedroom wall. Years later, Abby played alongside Mia on the U.S. Women's National Team.

Say It Like a Soccer Player

CORNER KICK: a kick taken from the corner of the field when the ball goes out of play over the goal line and was last touched by the defending team

DRIBBLE: a series of small kicks on the ball to move it around the field and past opponents

EXHIBITION GAME: a game played, in part, to prepare a team for a tournament. It can also be called a "friendly"

GOALKEEPER: a player whose main role is to prevent the opposing team from scoring goals. Sometimes this player is called the "goalie" or "keeper"

HAT TRICK: when one player scores three goals in a single game

VETERAN PLAYER: any player that is not new to a team or a first-year player

Bibliography

"Abby Wambach in Her Family's Eyes." US Soccer, 27 May 2015. www.ussoccer.com/womens-national-team/thanks-abby/in-her-familys-eyes.

Armour, Nancy. "Armour: Abby Wambach's Impact on Soccer Immense." *USA Today*, 16 Dec. 2015. www.usatoday.com/story/sports/soccer/2015/12/15/abby-wambach-leader-women-retirement/77387310.

Chavez, Bob. "Mercy Gives Up 3-Goal Lead, Loses in 'A' Final." *Democrat and Chronicle*, 16 Nov. 1997, pp. 1D–4D. Newspapers.com, 5. https://www.newspapers.com/image/136306113/?terms=-democrat%2Band%2Bchronicle%2C%2Bmercy%2Bhigh%2Bschool%2Bsoccer%2Bstate%2B-championship.

Fontela, Jonah. "Abby Wambach—We're Not Worthy." US Soccer, 17 Sept. 2019. www.ussoccer.com/stories/2019/09/abby-wambach-were-not-worthy.

Foudy, Julie. "Abby Wambach on Scoring Her 100th USWNT Goal in Her Hometown." March 30, 2020. ESPN FC. YouTube video, 8:33. www.youtube.com/watch?v=PFCUHjKzIkM.

Grant, Kristin. "Hometown Hero: Abby Wambach." *Reporter*, 5 Feb. 2016. reporter.rit.edu/sports/hometown-hero-abby-wambach.

Mahoney, Ridge. "Wambach Seeks Redemption." Soccer America, 7 Sept. 2007. www.socceramerica.com/publications/article/23354/wambach-seeks-redemption.html.

Rogers, Martin. "USA's Wambach Was Bred for This Moment." Yahoo Sports, 15 July 2011, 1. news.yahoo.com/usa-wambach-bred-moment-185800901--sow.html.

U.S. Soccer. "#OTD: Abby Wambach 100th Goal." Facebook Watch, U.S. Soccer, 19 July 2020. https://news.yahoo.com/news/usa-wambach-bred-moment-185800901--sow.html?fr=sycsrp_catchall.

"USWNT—OUCH! Abby Wambach Breaks Her Leg vs. Brazil." March 20, 2017. USWNT Classics. YouTube video, 13:07. www.youtube.com/watch?v=8U0-_dlBZ_c.

Wambach, Abby. *Forward: A Memoir*. New York: Dey St., 2016.